Woodlands

Charlotte Guillain

www.raintreepublishers.co.uk
Visit our website to find out more information about Raintree books.

To order:
☎ Phone 0845 6044371
▤ Fax +44 (0) 1865 312263
⊠ Email myorders@capstonepub.co.uk

Customers from outside the UK please telephone +44 1865 312262

Edited by Charlotte Guillain, Nancy Dickmann, and Catherine Veitch
Designed by Joanna Hinton-Malivoire
Picture research by Elizabeth Alexander and Ruth Blair
Original illustrations © Capstone Global Library
Production by Victoria Fitzgerald
Originated by Capstone Global Library Ltd
Printed and bound in China by Leo Paper Products

ISBN 978 0 431 17240 8
14 13 12 11 10
10 9 8 7 6 5 4 3 2 1

British Library Cataloguing in Publication Data
Guillain, Charlotte.
Woodlands. -- (Nature trails)
577.3-dc22

Acknowledgements
We would like to thank the following for permission to reproduce photographs: Corbis pp. **10** (© Peter Carlsson/Etsa), **23** (© Anne Laird), **25** (© Stefan Meyers); FLPA p. **4-5** (© Erica Olsen); iStockphoto pp. **6** (© Merijn van der Vliet), **7** (© Lukasz Kulicki), **13** (© Hans Laubel), **14** (© Philip Toy), **15** (© Rolf Robischon), **16**, **17** (© Anna Milkova), **18** (© Laurie Knight), **19** (© Henrik Larsson), **21** (© Gary Forsyth), **22** (© Torsten Stahlberg), **24** (© Valerie Crafter), **26** (© Keith Robertson), **27**; © PhotoDisc. 1993 p. **8 left** (Photolink); © PhotoDisc. 1998 pp. **8 right** (Life File. Andrew Ward), **9 right** (Life File. Andrew Ward); Punchstock p. **9 left** (Stockbyte).

Cover photograph of Rostrevor forest reproduced with permission of Corbis (© Richard Cummins).

The publisher would like to thank Emma Shambrook for her assistance in the preparation of this book.

Every effort has been made to contact copyright holders of material reproduced in this book. Any omissions will be rectified in subsequent printings if notice is given to the publisher.

All the internet addresses (URLs) given in this book were valid at the time of going to press. However, due to the dynamic nature of the Internet, some addresses may have changed or ceased to exist since publication. While the author and publishers regret any inconvenience this may cause readers, no responsibility for any such changes can be accepted by either the author or the publishers.

Contents

Any words appearing in the text in bold, **like this**, are explained in the glossary.

What is a woodland?

A woodland is an area of land with many trees growing together. In a woodland there is some space between the trees so plants and **shrubs** grow on the ground below.

A woodland is a type of **habitat**. A habitat is a place where animals and plants live. Many different animals and plants live in British woodlands.

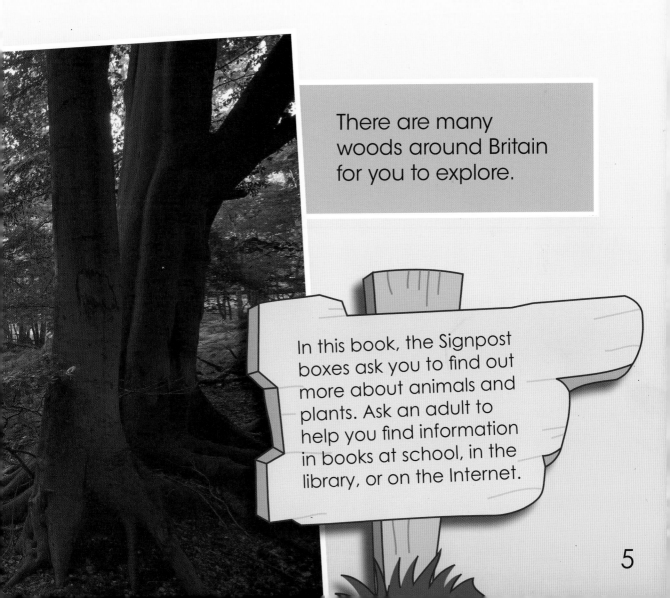

There are many woods around Britain for you to explore.

In this book, the Signpost boxes ask you to find out more about animals and plants. Ask an adult to help you find information in books at school, in the library, or on the Internet.

Different woodlands

There are two main types of trees in woodlands. **Broadleaved** trees have broad, flat leaves that drop off in the summer and autumn. Seeds and fruits grow on these trees in the summer.

Coniferous trees do not lose their leaves in winter. Their leaves are either long needles or small scales. **Cones** grow on coniferous trees.

Changing woodlands

Broadleaved trees change as the seasons change. In the spring, **blossom** grows on the branches of some trees. As the weather gets warmer, leaves start to bud and by the summer the trees are covered with leaves.

blossom

spring

summer

In the autumn, the leaves on broadleaved trees start to change colour, from green to yellows, reds, and oranges. Then the leaves fall from the trees. The tree branches are bare in winter.

autumn

winter

Exploring a woodland

Exploring woodland is easy and lots of fun. You can look for plants and animals in the soil and under fallen leaves and sticks, on the bark of trees, and on tree branches.

What to take with you

- ✓ A notebook and pencil
- ✓ A magnifying glass
- ✓ A soft brush to clean tree bark
- ✓ A digital camera

STAY SAFE

- Never disturb woodland animals or pull up plants.
- If you move logs or stones to look underneath, always put them back in the same place.
- Do not remove any part of a tree that is growing, such as branches, leaves, or bark.

Woodland trees

There are many different types of trees in British woodlands. Common **broadleaved** trees are oak, alder, ash, beech, and horse chestnut. You will also often see **coniferous** trees such as Scots pine, Douglas fir, and yew.

Coniferous trees make seeds in cones. The cones keep the seeds safe until they are ready to fall.

Broadleaved trees make seeds that grow inside fruits. There are lots of different types of fruit from sycamore "helicopters" to acorns and berries.

acorn

Woodland flowers and plants

Many different types of flower grow in woodlands. Flowers that like damp ground and shade grow well in this **habitat**. In the spring the ground can be covered in bluebells. You might also see wood anemones at this time of year.

bluebells

Foxgloves grow in woodland during the summer. In the winter you can often find snowdrops. Also look out for ferns in woodland, as they grow well in damp, shady places.

ferns

foxglove

Can you find out some more about woodland plants?

- wood sorrel
- primrose
- shrubs, such as hazel, hawthorn, and holly

Fungi, lichen, and moss

Fungi, such as mushrooms and toadstools, also like to grow in damp, dark places. You might find fungi on the ground in woodland or growing on tree trunks. Fungi get their food from dead plants and animals.

STAY SAFE

- Only touch wild fungus if an adult can tell you it is safe. Some fungi are **poisonous**.
- Always wash your hands after touching fungi.

Fungi make the soil good for trees to grow.

Lichen is a mixture of fungi and **algae**.

You can see **lichen** on tree trunks, branches, and stones. It can be white, green, brown, or orange. **Moss** also grows in clumps on the trees and ground.

Woodland minibeasts

There are many insects and other minibeasts in a woodland **habitat**. Minibeasts can find food and places to hide among the rotting leaves and wood and under tree bark.

Woodlice like dark, damp places and can often be found under stones or logs.

stag beetle

Slugs and snails and many beetles can be found on the ground in woodland, among the **leaf litter**. Look out for centipedes hunting for other minibeasts to eat.

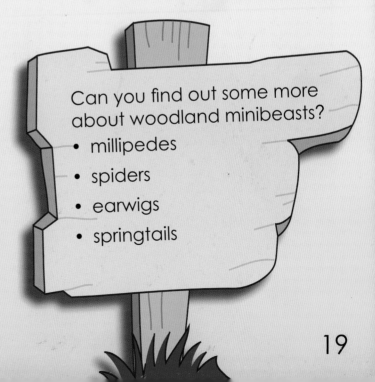

Can you find out some more about woodland minibeasts?

- millipedes
- spiders
- earwigs
- springtails

Woodland birds

Many birds live in a woodland **habitat**. These birds feed on the many minibeasts and seeds that live and grow in woods. Some birds live in British woodlands all year round, such as wood pigeons, tree creepers, woodpeckers, and tawny owls.

A woodland food chain

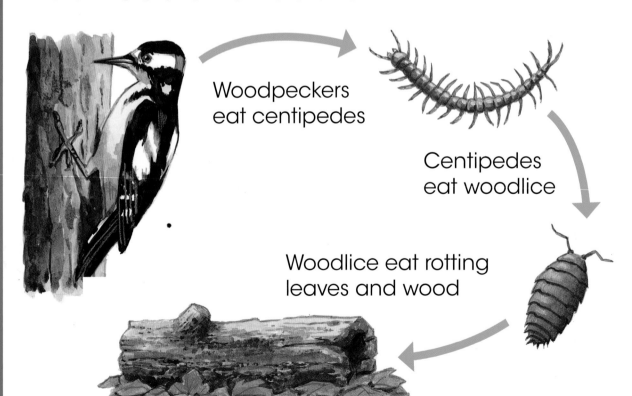

Woodpeckers eat centipedes

Centipedes eat woodlice

Woodlice eat rotting leaves and wood

tawny owl

In spring many birds arrive back in Britain after spending the winter in warmer places. You might spot chiffchaffs, willow warblers, and wood warblers. If you are very lucky you might hear a cuckoo.

Small mammals

Many bats make their homes in the very old trees found in woodland.

Tree branches, trunks, and roots make good homes and hiding places for small **mammals**. Many are very hard to spot because they are **nocturnal** or very shy, such as wood mice and dormice.

Red squirrels are now only found in parts of Britain, such as Scotland, the Lake District, and the Isle of Wight. In other areas you are more likely to see grey squirrels.

You can spot a pine marten by the yellow or white patch of fur on its neck.

Can you find out some more about small woodland mammals?

- shrews

- weasels

- voles

Large mammals

Larger mammals also make their homes in woodlands. Badgers and foxes are **nocturnal**, so they can be hard to see. You can look out for their footprints or **droppings**. You might spot the pathways that they follow every night to search for food.

You might spot a badger's sett or a fox hole.

red deer

If you stay quiet you may see deer in woodland. Deer hoofprints are easy to recognize with two toes on each foot. Look out for trees where deer have scratched and rubbed off the bark.

Woodlands in danger

Much of the woodland that used to cover Britain has been cut down for farming and building. When woodland disappears, so do all the animals and plants that live there. We need woodlands to help keep our air clean and our countryside beautiful.

Sometimes woodland is cut down to build new roads.

You can help protect woodlands by taking care when you visit woods. Always leave things as you find them and never leave litter behind because this can hurt animals and birds.

More things to do

There are a lot more things you can do in woodlands.

Count and record

Can you count some of the different signs that there are animals and birds in a woodland? Record them in a **tally chart** like this one.

Sign	Number spotted
Footprints	II
Droppings	III
Fur	I
Feathers	HH I
Nests	II

Bark rubbing

Different types of tree have different patterns on their bark. Take bark rubbings to keep a record of what different tree bark looks like:

1 Choose a tree and brush off the surface of a small area of bark.

2 Use masking tape to hold a sheet of paper steady against the bark.

3 Gently rub the paper with the side of a wax crayon so the pattern shows through.

4 Carefully remove the paper and make a note of the type of tree the bark is from and the colour of the bark.

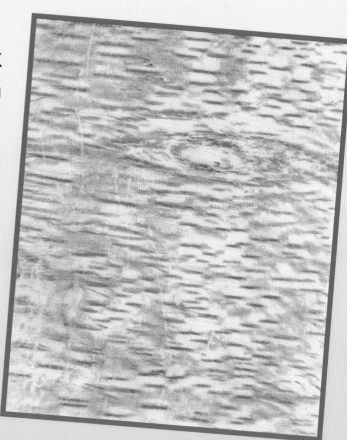

Glossary

alga simple plants that grow in water or damp places

algae plural of alga

blossom flower, usually on a fruit tree

broadleaved trees that lose all their leaves in autumn. They usually have wide, flat leaves.

cone part of a coniferous tree that holds seeds

coniferous trees that do not lose all their leaves at the same time. They usually have leaves like needles.

droppings animal poo

fungus simple plants such as mushrooms, toadstools, and mould

fungi plural of fungus

habitat natural home of a group of plants and animals

leaf litter rotting leaves and other dead plant material on the ground

lichen mixture of fungus and algae that grows as a crust on branches or rocks

mammal group of animals that includes humans. All mammals feed their babies on milk and have some fur or hair on their bodies.

moss small green plants that grow in damp places

poisonous chemical that can damage or kill living things

nocturnal animal or bird that is active at night

shrub small, woody plant

tally chart table that shows the number of something. A tally chart helps with counting.

Find out more

Books to read

Spotter's Guides: Woodland Life, Sue Jacquemier and Sarah Kahn (Usborne, 2009)

Wild Britain: Woodlands, Louise and Richard Spilsbury (Heinemann Library, 2001)

Websites and organizations

Woodland Trust
www.woodlandtrust.org.uk
The Woodland Trust website has many activities for you to try. You can also search for a wood to visit near you.

RSPB
www.rspb.org.uk
On the RSPB website you can identify the birds you see and find out more about looking after woodland wildlife.

Index